The Navigation Way

A hundred mile towpath walk around Birmingham and the West Midlands

by Peter Groves

Canal sketches by Zette Braithwaite

D1439473

Tetradon Publications Ltd

The Long Boat Public House on Brindley Walk, Birmingham

FOREWORD

There are now many long distance footpaths in Britain, but the route described in this book is unique in being located in the centre of a highly industrialised region. The West Midlands is richly endowed in a variety of ways and Peter Groves has utilised two of its valuable recreational assets — its fine countryside and its extensive canal system — to devise this walk which will, I hope, give pleasure to the many who appreciate the attractions and benefits of exploring Britain on foot.

The canals were the 'arteries' of the Industrial Revolution and the observant walker who follows this route will learn much about the industrial history of Birmingham and the West Midlands and will, I feel sure, be in a better position to appreciate the contribution that the region has in the past made towards the prosperity of Britain.

Chairman, Birmingham Civic Society

The drawings on pages viii, 8, 19 and 29 are from *Canals in Towns* by Lewis Braithwaite and are reproduced by kind permission of the publishers, A & C Black Ltd., and the author.

NETHERTON TUNNEL (Section 3)

The Netherton tunnel has recently been closed for extensive repairs. To reach the other end using public transport, walk north-west, along the road running parallel to the canal by which you approach the tunnel, until you reach the A461 at Dudley Port. From here take the 74 bus into Dudley bus station. Then take the 140 bus as far as Warrens Hall Park and walk south-west from the park entrance. A tall chimney marks the end of the tunnel and provides a good landmark.

PREFACE

In 1976 my wife and I decided that we wanted to do some mid-week evening walking. The canals seemed attractive and readily accessible and so, in the glorious summer of that year, we embarked on a number of enjoyable excursions along the towpaths. But, although we met anglers, runners and people on boats, we were struck by the absence of other walkers. Were they all on the Pennine Way or the Offa's Dyke Path? Or did Midlands walkers — and we knew that there were many of them — not realise what was available so close at hand. It seemed a pity that such a valuable asset was so little used — but I hope that this book will help to introduce more people to the pleasures of towpath walking.

It would be foolish to claim that the route that I have described compares for excitement and scenic beauty with the national long distance footpaths. But much of it passes through fine walking country, especially the sections along the Worcester & Birmingham, the Stourbridge and the Staffordshire & Worcestershire canals. And all of it is extremely interesting, especially to the observant walker who want to know more about, for example, the history, the geography, the bird and animal life, and the industrial past (and present) of this part of the West Midlands.

In the book I have described the route, given a little history, explained some features of the canals, and mentioned some of the things that I have found interesting. A detailed description of everything along the route would require many more pages than there are in this short guide. But much of the fun in this kind of walk is in spotting things yourself and in trying to work out what they are, or what they mean, in the context of the present or of the past. I hope that you will enjoy it as much as I have done.

I am very grateful to Zette Braithwaite for her delightful sketches of canal scenes. Also, I am indebted to three people who have read and commented on the manuscript. They are:

Miss Dorothy McCulla, Head of the Local Studies Section of Birmingham Central Library, who was especially helpful with old maps and various aspects of local history;

Mr Lewis Braithwaite, Staff Tutor in the Department of Extra-Mural Studies in the University of Birmingham and author of *Canals in Towns,* who gave me much useful information and, at an excellent series of evening lectures, taught me a great deal about the canal system;

and my wife Jean, who took great pains to scrutinise all that I wrote, and corrected my English, and my obscurities and illogicalities.

Peter Groves
Sandwell, West Midlands. 1978

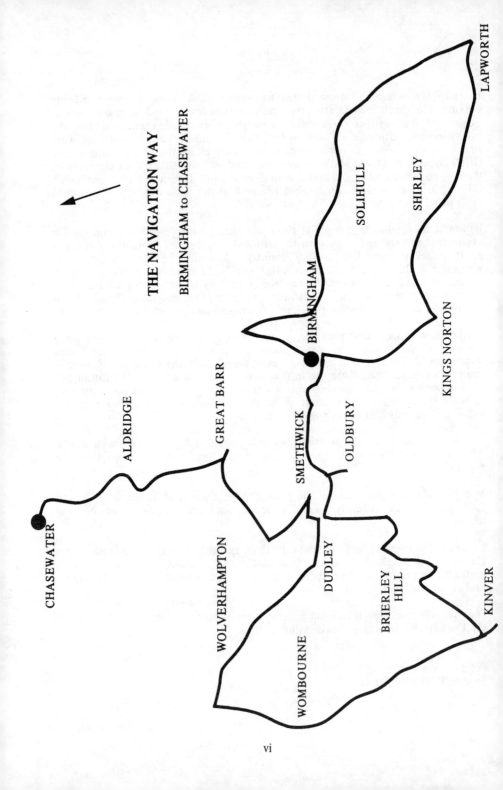

THE NAVIGATION WAY

BIRMINGHAM to CHASEWATER

LAPWORTH

SOLIHULL

SHIRLEY

BIRMINGHAM

KINGS NORTON

ALDRIDGE

GREAT BARR

SMETHWICK

OLDBURY

CHASEWATER

WOLVERHAMPTON

DUDLEY

WOMBOURNE

BRIERLEY HILL

KINVER

INTRODUCTION

This book is divided into seven sections, each describing a walk averaging about fifteen miles. These have convenient starting and finishing places and will enable the experienced walker to complete the hundred miles in a week. However, there is nothing sacred about this division and, if your walking ambitions are more modest, you will have no difficulty in dividing the route into shorter units. Much of it can be done in the evenings during the summer months.

The distance of one hundred miles is as measured on the Ordnance Survey map. One would expect the true walking distance to be rather greater than this.

There is plenty of public transport in the region, and there are few points where you are far from a West Midlands or Midland Red bus. A bus map and set of timetables, available from WMPTE and Midland Red travel centres will be helpful.

Food and refreshment should present no problems as there are plenty of pubs along the way — and the West Midlands is noted for its real ale. Most pubs provide food, though not always at weekends, so it would be wise to have something in reserve if you are walking on a Saturday or Sunday.

An Ordnance Survey map is always useful — not that you are likely to lose your way along the canals, but because it will supplement the strip maps in this book and help you to see more clearly where you are in relation to towns and villages. And it may sometimes be helpful at the end of a walk when you are looking for a bus route. The Ordnance Survey 1:50 000 sheet 139 covers the entire walk, with the exception of the short section between Stourton and Kinver.

Good footwear is desirable, especially after rain when parts of the towpath may be very muddy. In a few short sections the towpath is rather overgrown and here an anorak or walking jacket will protect you from scratches.

For the Netherton tunnel (section 3) a reliable torch is essential (and a spare battery if you are nervous!). Stout footwear also is essential because the path usually contains some very large puddles.

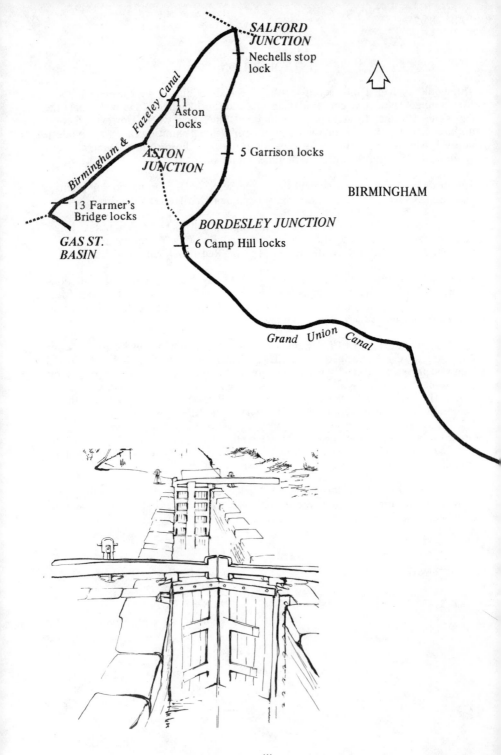

SALFORD
JUNCTION

Nechells stop
lock

Birmingham & Fazeley Canal

1 Aston locks

ASTON JUNCTION

5 Garrison locks

BIRMINGHAM

13 Farmer's Bridge locks

GAS ST. BASIN

BORDESLEY JUNCTION

6 Camp Hill locks

Grand Union Canal

1. BIRMINGHAM TO KNOWLE

Our walk starts in the centre of Birmingham at the Worcester Bar basin, generally known as Gas Street basin. Gas Street is off Broad Street and access to the basin is through a doorway in the wall a little way along on the left. This is the centre of the extensive network of canals which penetrate this part of the West Midlands. Birmingham, it is said, has more miles of canals than Venice and our walk includes most of these.

As you go down to the basin from the street, note, underfoot, the characteristic pattern of brickwork. The raised bricks are to prevent horses from slipping, a reminder of the days when canal boats were horsedrawn. We shall meet this pattern many times, especially under bridges.

Although much altered in recent years, the basin is still a fascinating place with its gaily decorated narrow boats, its old canal buildings (though some old warehouses have, unfortunately, been demolished) and its views of some of the fine new buildings that characterise modern Birmingham.

We set off west, under the Broad Street tunnel, and along the Birmingham Canal, but almost immediately turn north-east onto the Birmingham & Fazeley Canal opened in 1789 (signposted Nottingham 58, Lincoln 114, Leeds 152). However, we have first to go a little way along the Birmingham Canal to cross to the other side by a bridge marked Horseley Iron Works 1827. This is a *roving bridge;* that is, one that takes a towpath across a canal.

On our right we soon see the modern canalside development that won for the City of Birmingham a Civic Trust award in 1970. Some 18th century cottages have been modernised (one is an interesting canal shop); a fine new pub, the Long Boat, and some blocks of flats have been built; and the canal side has been laid out as a walk, named after James Brindley (1716-1772) who was responsible for most of the early English canals. Unfortunately, at the time of writing, there is no direct access from

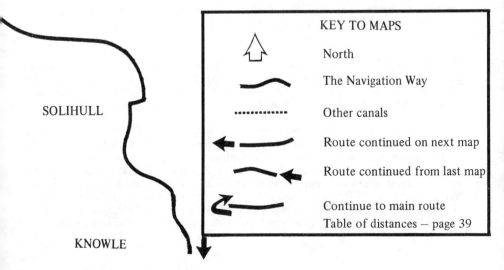

SOLIHULL

KNOWLE

KEY TO MAPS

North

The Navigation Way

Other canals

Route continued on next map

Route continued from last map

Continue to main route
Table of distances — page 39

1

the towpath. However, if you go back to the canal junction, you should be able to go through the car park there and over Tindal Bridge. This will bring you out by the canal shop.

The Birmingham Canal and the Birmingham & Fazeley Canal companies were amalgamated in 1784 to form the 'Birmingham and Birmingham & Fazeley Canal Company'. This cumbersome title was changed to the Birmingham Canal Navigations (BCN) in 1794. Other canals were subsequently incorporated into the BCN, and by 1865 the Company owned about 160 miles of canal, just over 100 miles of which remain.

We now come to the flight of 13 Farmer's Bridge Locks, almost roofed over in places by the many bridges in this central area of Birmingham and by a number of new buildings which have been built out over the canal. In front is the Post Office tower and then one of the massive arches of Brunel's old Snow Hill Station. At the first lock there is a characteristic toll house to your left.

Beside the locks you will see *side pounds*, small reservoirs to the side rather than in their usual position between locks. A *pound* is the stretch of water between two locks. In its heyday this was an extremely busy canal, the locks working 24 hours a day. The remains of gas lamps at locks 2, 3 and 7 remind us of night working. This was a notorious bottleneck and, because there was no room to build a parallel flight of locks (as was done, for example, at Smethwick), this bottleneck could not be relieved until the Warwick and Birmingham and the Tame Valley canals were built.

At the iron Barker Bridge (dated 1842) you will see a sign warning of underground high voltage cables. One important use of the canal towpaths is to provide a convenient route for gas and electricity services and, in the steel making areas, oxygen. In some of the bridges and walls bordering the canal, red doors provide access for the fire services. Canals are a valuable source of water for firefighting, and you will meet these doors frequently in towns.

On the next bridge (Lancaster Street) there is an interesting piece of cast-ironwork - the back of a Victorian urinal, still in working order. But there is no access from the canal.

At Aston Junction the Digbeth branch canal enters from the right. Look out for the fine cast-iron bridge (Horseley Ironworks 1828). South from here you can see the University of Aston, marked by a radio mast on the roof. This is Birmingham's newer, technological, university, which gained its charter in 1966.

We continue north-east down the flight of 11 Aston locks. These locks, and those that we passed at Farmer's Bridge, are characteristic of the BCN in having single bottom gates. Bottom gates are usually double: this is because top gates are mostly submerged when they are opened and so are 'floating', whereas bottom gates are mostly out of the water and therefore much heavier to handle. These locks are narrow locks, seven feet wide, and able only to accommodate a single *narrow boat,* the most common British canal boat with a beam of just under seven feet. At the second lock there is a lock-keepers cottage, with access to the road and a pub.

This section is somewhat unprepossessing, going through ragged industrial development and much derelict land. But the canal architecture is interesting and there is much to remind us of the days when this was one of the main arteries of commerce. There are many old canal arms and basins (shown by old bridges) which originally provided a direct connection between factory and canal. In 1839 it was reported that there were *'nearly 70 Steam Engines and about 124 Wharfs and Works ... seated on the Banks of the Canals, between Farmer's Bridge and Aston'.*

Just before lock 9 there is an old wharf linked by an arm over which the towpath passes. As you approach lock 10, look out for a wall, to the left, with old millstones built into its base.

At lock 10 there is another lock keeper's cottage. To the left of the lock you will see the planks used for *stopping* the canal - necessary if a section has to be drained for repairs or, where there is an embankment, for stopping the flow of water if there should be a burst. During the war various sections of the canals were stopped at night as a precaution against bursts that might be caused by bombing. You will see *stop planks* at various points along your walk. Below the bottom gate of this lock are the slots into which the planks are fitted.

By the bottom gate of the lock there is an interesting cantilever bridge which is anchored only at the far side, the near side having a gap of a few inches through which the towrope could pass. Just beyond, is a fine six storied building, while to your right you have the opportunity to peer through the windows of a factory to see the activity within.

Six-storied mill in Aston, Birmingham on the Birmingham and Fazeley canal.

3

A fleet of narrow boats and cruisers indicates that we are near to Salford Junction which we meet after crossing an attractive 1780s brick and stonework aqueduct over the heavily polluted river Tame. Salford Junction was an important part of the canal system with the Tame Valley Canal (which we shall meet later on our walk) to the north-west, the Birmingham & Fazeley continuing to the east, and the Grand Union to the south. We shall turn right onto the Grand Union (signposted Warwick) and follow this b,ck into the heart of Birmingham. But first you might like to leave the canal for a few minutes (there is an exit to the road a few yards along the Tame Valley Canal) and stand in the centre of the open space below the Gravelly Hill motorway interchange *('Spaghetti Junction')* and reflect on the changes in transport that have taken place since the beginning of the canal age. There is a pub handy if you are in need of refreshment.

This section of the Grand Union was opened in 1844 (it was then the Birmingham & Warwick Junction canal) and it relieved pressure on the Birmingham & Fazeley by acting as a by-pass to the 13 Farmer's Bridge and 11 Aston locks that we saw earlier. The first bridge is numbered 110: you will see that, as on many canals, bridges on the Grand Union, with the exception of the newer ones, have numbers.

We cross the river Tame again and are soon back in a heavily industrialised area, a fact which is readily apparent, not only to our eyes but also to our ears and nose. The first lock is Nechells *stop lock* which had a fall of only six inches and was designed to control the flow of water between canals. Stop locks were particularly important when the canals were owned by private, and competing, companies. Water supply was a perennial problem on many canals, and companies had no wish to provide free water for their competitors. The gates of Nechells lock are now chained open.

Beneath our feet a high pressure gas main now accompanies the electricity main.

After crossing the culverted river Rea, Saltley reservoir can be seen to the left. This supports a considerable amount of wild life, even though it is in the middle of such a heavily industrialised area. If you are a naturalist you will find much to interest you here, although it is rather difficult to get a good view from the towpath.

The five Garrison locks now take us up about 35 feet. These have the more conventional double bottom gates for we are now no longer on the BCN. A lock keeper's cottage at the first lock provides access to the road.

There are many loading stages along this stretch of canal with rampways up to the road, though these are now mostly blocked off. The Grand Union canal goes to London and was of great importance to Birmingham industry.

We soon pass under the main railway line to London and are back into an area dominated by bridges. There is a particularly fine view of these looking south from bridge 104.

At Bordesley junction we meet the Warwick and Birmingham Canal. Look out for the deep grooves in the iron bridge here, caused by the continual passage of towropes. You will frequently meet grooves like this, especially at bridges, and their depth gives some indication of how heavily the canals were used by horse-drawn

4

boats. If you wish, you can return to Gas Street from here, passing the Warwick Bar with its stop lock and many signs of earlier canal activity, ascending the six Ashted locks, through the short Ashted tunnel, and then turning left onto the Birmingham & Fazeley at Aston Junction.

Our route, however, continues along the Grand Union, still criss-crossed by road and railway bridges, and ascending the six narrow Camp Hill locks. Beyond, we move into the suburbs of Birmingham, and the surroundings gradually change from industrial to residential and then, later, to rural.

We soon pass the old Bordesley railway sidings on our left, now a park for new motor vehicles, followed by a large timber yard. Our route is now fairly uneventful though with signs of former activity in the old loading bays in the factory walls. Just before bridge 90 a fine clock tower, on a pub, can be seen to the right.

Soon we can see some of the first signs of the improvements to the Grand Union that were carried out, as an unemployment measure and with a Government grant, in the 1930s. Alongside some playing fields the canal bank has been rebuilt, with the date 1932 set into the concrete. A big modernisation programme dredged, piled, and widened the locks so that 15 foot wide barges could pass (the Camp Hill locks that we saw earlier are the last narrow locks on this canal). However, the work was never completed and an ambitious attempt to make the canals, once more, into an important part of Britain's transport system, failed.

The view now starts to open up with much vacant and derelict land. Just before the modern Tyseley waste disposal plan, an old rubbish tip is clearly an attraction to treasure seekers! An aqueduct takes us over the river Cole and we soon see signs of earlier large scale commercial activity with a big wharf just past bridge 88. By the towpath, posts marked 'WMGB Anode' remind us that the gas main is still below our feet, protected from corrosion by an electrochemical method.

Although now in the residential suburbs we still meet pockets of industry. There are some pleasant cuttings, unfortunately marred, in places, by rubbish. Houses are getting larger and, as we approach Solihull, we find residents starting to use the canal as a feature of their gardens. There is a very attractive garden in the grounds of the Gas Board headquarters.

Beyond Solihull we are in the real countryside (with fields and cattle!) and we pass through a delightful cutting. Bridge 78 is at Catherine de Barnes Heath: this appears on the original 1790s canal plan as Cat in the Barn Heath. There is a pub here named, appropriately, The Boat.

At bridge 77 there are stop planks, and a weir with a discharge to the river Blythe, which we later cross. Although canals frequently suffer from shortage of water, they can, in bad weather, suffer from an excess and weirs are necessary to prevent flooding. And, of course, the water coming down canals has to be discharged somewhere! There is also a sluice gate here which can be opened if necessary, for example, if there is a break in the embankment.

After bridge 73 the half timbered Grimshaw Hall can be seen to the right (though the view is rather obscured by trees in the summer) and then the square tower of Knowle church.

On page 16 is a copy of part of the original plan for the Warwick & Birmingham Canal: this can be seen, together with many other plans for Warwickshire canals, in the County Record Office in Warwick. The study of old maps is always a fascinating activity and if you can obtain plans like this they will provide added interest to your walk. You may like to compare the field and road pattern shown in our map with those that you can see from the canal. Although there have been changes, many a direct result of the building of the canal, much remains as it was. The roads are mostly unchanged. Some of the hedges still mark out the earlier field boundaries. Knowle Hall still exists; Henwood Hall is now Henwood Hall Farm, and Waterfield Hall is Waterfield Farm.

At Hern Field (now Heronfield) there were four fields showing the mediaeval pattern of strip cultivation. There do not seem to be any remaining traces of these strips, though perhaps the trained eye will be able to detect signs of ridge and furrow somewhere. The Black Boy public house appears to the south-east of its present position on the canal-side. It was rebuilt there, no doubt, to obtain the custom of the boatmen.

The map shows that there were originally six locks at Knowle. There are now only five and they are very different from those that we have seen so far on our walk. These were rebuilt and widened in the 1930s modernisation. However, remains of the earlier locks can be seen incorporated into the new.

Knowle is a convenient place to break our journey. There are buses to Solihull, and Dorridge railway station is about two miles distant.

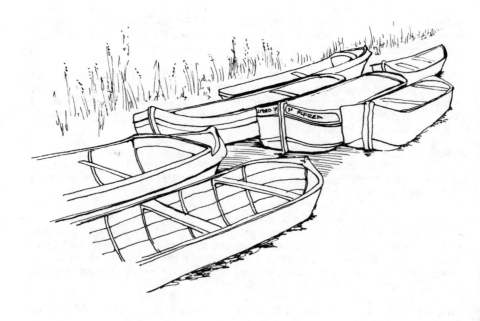

2. KNOWLE TO KINGS NORTON

We now continue, past the Knowle locks, remembering to refer to the old map on page 16 and the comments on this given in the last section.

We are here in good farming country and there are numerous opportunities for watching wild life. The canal contains many fresh water mussels, the shells of which can be found in the towpath where they have been deposited by dredging.

The towpath crosses to the right at bridge 67: this is easy to miss as it is possible to continue for a little way on the left. The next bridge is a *pipe bridge.* There are many of these to be seen on our walk and they carry various services over the canal. Unfortunately, most are eyesores, in marked contrast to the many elegant bridges constructed by the canal companies.

At bridge 66 a sign marks the boundary between the former Trent River Authority and the Severn River Authority (now merged). A study of a map will show that we are on the watershed between the two rivers. To the north, natural drainage is into the Trent through the rivers Rea, Cole and Blythe, all of which we have crossed To the south, drainage is to the Severn, through the rivers Alne, Arrow and Avon: later we shall cross some of the streams running into these.

Just past bridge 65 (where there is a pub with a traditional canal name, The Navigation Inn) we come to a branch that takes us to the Stratford-on-Avon canal. We turn to the right here, the towpath being on the left. However, the towpath walk going south along the Grand Union is very attractive and you might like to return here one day and walk the 8½ miles to Warwick.

The short branch from the Grand Union brings us, through one lock, to the Stratford-on-Avon canal. You will notice that we are now back to narrow locks. In the pound to the right of the lock is a 'graveyard' of old narrow boats. To the south the canal is the property of the National Trust whose canal office is at the junction. A plaque on the adjacent bridge records that: *'After 30 years of dereliction this canal was restored (1961-64) by volunteers, prisoners and servicemen, with the help of subscribers.'* A collection box here enables you to make a contribution to maintenance costs.

The Southern Stratford provides another very attractive walk and the 13½ miles should certainly be followed on some occasion. Our route goes to the north, but before leaving this very pleasant junction have a look at the barrel-roofed lock keeper's cottage which is typical of the southern section. There are several of these to be seen on the way to Stratford. The northern and southern sections are very different in style, having been constructed at different times (northern section opened 1802; southern section opened 1816). The northern section was important for the transport of Dudley coal which then went on to London along the Grand Union.

Another characteristic of the southern section is the *split bridge,* one of which you cross by the canal office, and which was designed to allow the towrope to pass through. These bridges were much cheaper to construct than the more conventional design, which has to be wide enough for the horse to pass underneath.

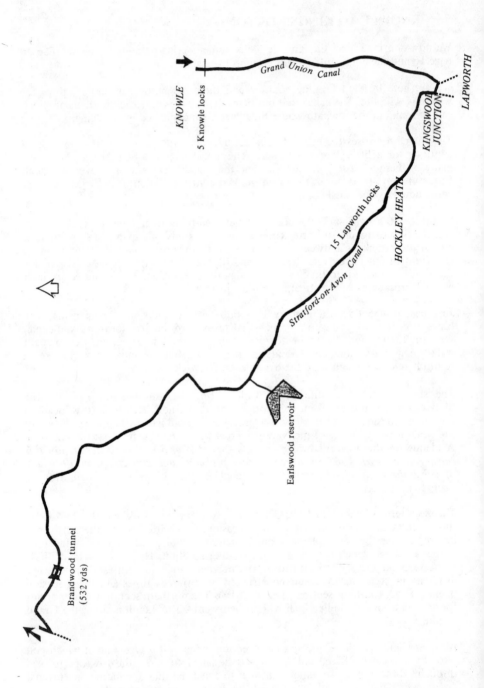

KNOWLE

5 Knowle locks

Grand Union Canal

KINGSWOOD JUNCTION

LAPWORTH

15 Lapworth locks

HOCKLEY HEATH

Stratford-on-Avon Canal

Earlswood reservoir

Brandwood tunnel
(532 yds)

We now climb about 74 feet by the Lapworth locks. At lock 14 there is a pub, The Boot (a corruption of The Boat?), and a split bridge (even though we are now on the northern section). Look out for marks of the towrope on this.

Bridges 28 and 26 are *lift bridges*, raised by windlasses. Signs under several bridges show that the boundary between the Severn and the Trent River Authorities now crosses the canal at several points, indicating the varying direction of the (natural) contours along the line of the (artificial) canal. Food and refreshment can be obtained at bridge 19 at the Blue Bell which is a cider house.

Approaching bridge 16 a high embankment takes us over a tributary of the river Blythe and we then see, to the left, a feeder from Earlswood reservoir. The three lakes of this make an attractive detour.

Near to Shirley station a brick aqueduct takes the canal over both road and river Cole. Shortly after, there is an old rubbish tip which is an attraction for collectors of Victorian bottles.

The route now becomes increasingly suburban, with signs of industry appearing near bridge 6. Once again we start to encounter rubbish, frequently tipped from gardens that back onto the canal. This often happens when houses are fenced off from the canal, though when fences are absent the residents incorporate the canal bank into their garden and make it into an attractive feature. The lesson to be drawn seems obvious.

After passing an old coal wharf just before the Alcester Road, we enter a pleasant cutting which leads to the Brandwood tunnel. There is no towpath and boats had to be *'legged'* through. The towpath climbs up to the road.

To rejoin the canal go straight across the island and down Brandwood Park Road. Turn left into Shelfield Road and then down the path on the right by the side of house number 11.

This entrance has, at some time, been blocked, presumably to keep children away from the canal. One can understand the anxiety of parents, though it might be more logical to fence off the roads which are so much more dangerous. But it is virtually impossible to keep children away from such an attractive play area and they will always find a way through fences. Fences, in fact, can sometimes prevent an adult from getting to the aid of a child in difficulties.

Arriving back onto the canal, note that the western end of the Brandwood tunnel is marked by a bust of Shakespeare, now somewhat decayed.

The junction with the Worcester and Birmingham Canal is marked by a stop lock with two interesting gates with cast iron columns and machinery. These are *'guillotine'* gates and were constructed in this way so that the water level on either side could be six inches or so higher than on the other. They are now permanently open. Ahead can be seen the spire of Kings Norton church. At the junction is a fine canal house with a characteristic bay window giving a good view of the canal, and clearly built for a more important official than a lock keeper.

We are now back in Birmingham and buses are not far away.

One of the guillotine gates of the Kings Norton stop lock. Stratford on Avon canal.

3. KINGS NORTON TO NETHERTON

Our route now turns north along the Worcester and Birmingham Canal. *Stop gates* can be seen under bridge 73 and under several other bridges as we make our way into Birmingham. We are clearly in a heavily industrialised area. A tall chimney to our right marks a refuse disposal plant: a foundry follows. To the left the remains of an old wharf can be seen. Engineering works, a medical supplies factory, a chocolate warehouse and a timber yard can all be seen from the pleasant grassy towpath. At Bournville, which we first recognise by the smell of chocolate, the railway joins us and remains our companion for the rest of the way into the city.

The canal passes through Cadbury's works. Just past the rebuilt Bournville station there is an old lift bridge which originally linked the two parts of the factory. To the right the old loading wharf is still used as a warehouse although the only boats now to be seen there are used for pleasure. To the left are some of the attractive houses, lawns and trees of the Bournville Village Trust, world famous as a pioneer garden city.

After passing under bridge 79, the Chamberlain Campanile (built in 1900) of the University of Birmingham can be seen to the right. At bridge 80 the huge Queen Elizabeth hospital is straight ahead. After the next railway bridge there is a fine view, from a high embankment, over the university. To the left is the new railway station, serving hospital and university.

As we approach the city centre the surroundings become increasingly attractive and there is a sharp contrast with the views that we had from the Birmingham & Fazeley and the Grand Union canals. This is a unique approach to a major British city, its park-like character being combined with fine views of some tall modern buildings. Much of the land that we pass through is part of the Calthorpe Estate which, by restrictive covenants, prevented the commercial and industrial exploitation of this part of Edgbaston.

After passing the Botanical Gardens on our left, we enter the short Edgbaston tunnel. At bridge 85, the Post Office tower, which we passed on our journey north, can be seen straight ahead. After passing the Accident Hospital on our right, the canal makes a sharp left turn over an aqueduct and we are back at Gas Street basin. Originally, the Worcester and Birmingham Canal was separated from the Birmingham canal by a strip of land (the Worcester Bar) and goods had to be carried across here from one canal to the other. This unsatisfactory situation, which was to the financial benefit of the Birmingham canal, was only resolved by an Act of Parliament in 1815, as a result of which heavy compensation tolls were paid to the Birmingham company and a stop lock was built. The gates of this are now kept permanently open.

From this point you can pick out several of the more prominent City buildings, including the Clock Tower ('Big Brum') on the Council House, the tall and elegant pre-cast concrete ATV building, the rounded sides of the new Birmingham Repertory Theatre, the fine tower of St Philips and, immediately to its right, the oddly-shaped National Westminster House.

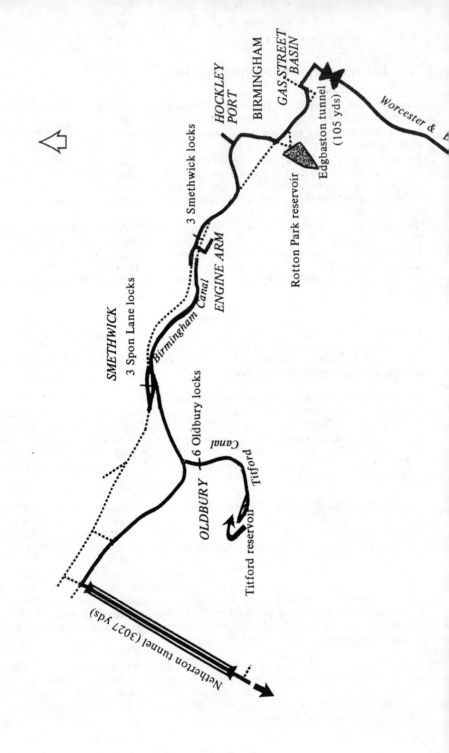

BIRMINGHAM

GAS STREET BASIN

HOCKLEY PORT

Edgbaston tunnel (105 yds)

Rotton Park reservoir

Worcester &

3 Smethwick locks

ENGINE ARM

Birmingham Canal

SMETHWICK

3 Spon Lane locks

6 Oldbury locks

OLDBURY

Titford Canal

Titford reservoir

Netherton tunnel (3027 yds)

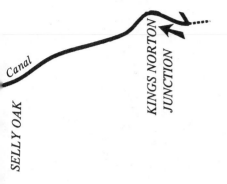

SELLY OAK   *Canal*   *KINGS NORTON JUNCTION*

We are now about to set out along another exit from the city and one of the most interesting historically.

The first canal in Birmingham was built by James Brindley who was authorised in 1768 to build a line to meet the Staffordshire & Worcestershire at Aldersley Junction, north of Wolverhampton. The first section was opened a year later and connected the collieries at Wednesbury with Birmingham. The remainder was completed over the next three years.

To keep earth moving costs to a minimum, and because the science of soil mechanics was little understood, the early canals of Brindley's time avoided deep cuttings and embankments and wandered along contour lines. When a hill was encountered that could not be gone around, a tunnel was built or else the canal was taken over the hill by means of locks. This canal was typical of such, wandering so much that it took 22½ miles to reach Aldersley, distant only 13 miles as the crow flies. Twelve locks were required to take it over Smethwick hill, six up and six down, a reservoir being built to supply water at the summit. An attempt was made to cut a tunnel but this failed due to the loose sandy nature of the ground.

During the next fifty to sixty years various improvements were made. John Smeaton, designer of the Eddystone Lighthouse, was employed to lower the summit by means of a cutting which removed six of the locks, and also to build a parallel flight of locks at the Birmingham end to increase the flow of traffic. A small natural lake at Rotton Park was extended to become a reservoir. Steam engines were installed at various points to pump up water from the lower level and then, between 1825 and 1838, improvements designed by Thomas Telford shortened the route by some seven miles by means of cuttings and embankments. We shall see much of this work on the section that we are now about to walk.

We set off as before, under the Broad Street tunnel, on which there used to be a church, demolished in 1978. We turn left in the direction signposted Wolverhampton, Liverpool, Manchester. The first roving bridge that we encounter goes over the Oozells Street loop, which was part of Brindley's original route, the straight section that we are following being due to Telford.

Approaching Edgbaston tunnel. Worcester and Birmingham Canal.

This canal has towpaths on both sides but we will cross over to the right hand side. There we soon meet some new, well designed, municipal housing with pleasant gardens facing the towpath, though separated from it by a fence. This imaginative scheme has transformed an originally derelict area and it is to be hoped that the city will make more good use of its many waterways.

Just past the Monument Lane bridge, another Brindley loop goes off to the left: this also serves as a *feeder*, bringing in water from the Rotton Park reservoir. When this rejoins the main line another Brindley loop (the Soho loop), which we shall follow goes off to the right, Telford's line continuing straight ahead through a cutting. As the Soho loop winds around we have some good views of the city and can see some of the new housing developments. A short branch to the right will take us to Hockley Port, now being redeveloped for use by pleasure craft.

The factories to our left are on an island between the main line and the Soho loop. They mostly present a decayed face to the canal although one has laid out a pleasant grassed area, overlooked by a curious tall chimney.

A tall wall to our right, overtopped by trees, surrounds the secluded grounds of All Saints Hospital. Following this is Winson Green Prison.

As we rejoin Telford's main line, an island can be seen in the middle of the canal on which there was, originally, a toll office. There are several other such islands on the BCN.

The smoke from the Smethwick foundries can now be seen ahead and at Rabone Lane Bridge we encounter the activity going on within one of them. There have been foundries in this area for almost 300 years and, to our right as we come up to the bridge, is Boulton and Watt's Soho foundry where the first effective steam engines were made. Some of the old buildings are still standing.

After two roving bridges (Horseley Iron Works 1828) Telford's main line carries straight on, but we branch off to the right along Brindley's canal. At the next bridge there is a pub, the Old Navigation, with, in the lounge, some interesting paintings of the old canals.

The three Smethwick locks now lift the canal 20 feet. These locks are Smeaton's, the parallel flight on the far side having been demolished. However, some traces of the third lock are still visible.

A little further on, the 'Engine Arm' branches to the left, crossing Telford's line by a fine iron aqueduct, built in 1825. There was originally a pumping engine here, one of Boulton and Watt's first, installed in 1770 to pump water back up the locks to save the supply from the reservoir. The engine is now in the Birmingham Museum of Science and Industry. We will cross the aqueduct and take the short walk through the factories to the end of the arm where the inlet, feeding water from the Rotten Park reservoir, can just be seen.

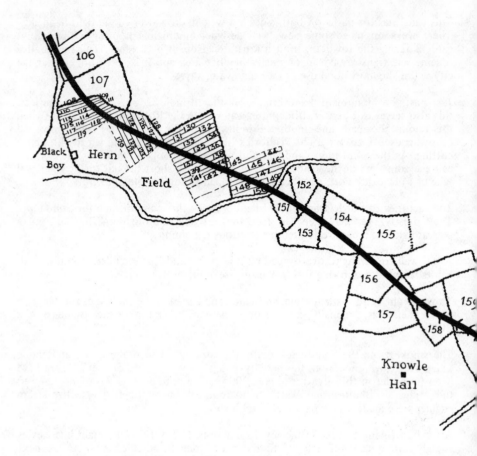

Copy of part of the deposited plan, dated 1792, for the Warwick & Birmingham Canal, held in the Warwick County Record Office (ref. QS111/4).

The numbers refer to the owners of the plots of land through which the canal was to pass.

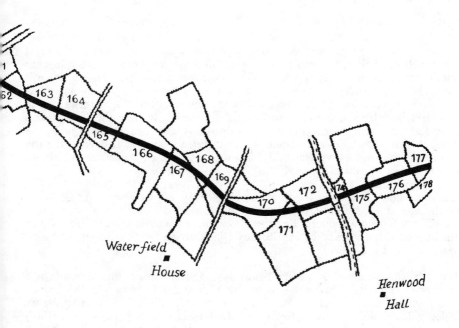

Returning across the acqueduct we continue north-west, Telford's main line running parallel and below us through a deep cutting. Past Brasshouse bridge is the old pumphouse which was built in 1892 to replace the Engine Arm pumping station. Above, to the right, a footpath can be seen, with access at the end of the Rabone Lane bridge. This marks the line of Brindley's original summit level canal. If you walk a little way along this footpath you will have a fine view of the two cuttings, first Smeaton's of 1790 and then Telford's of 1825. One can reflect on the vast amount of labour required to move all the soil for these cuttings, remembering that the labourers had only hand tools.

Let us now descend to Telford's line by steps just past the engine house. We find ourselves in a pleasant deep sided cutting covered with wild flowers and blackberry bushes, and it is difficult to appreciate that we are so close to Smethwick industry. Look out for wild life: you may well see a kestrel hovering overhead.

The Galton tunnel takes us under a new road. This is not a tunnel in the conventional sense since the concrete archwork was constructed before the soil of the embankment was dumped on top of it. Emerging from the tunnel we see Telford's fine 150 feet span Galton Bridge, 71 feet above the water, built in 1829. Unfortunately, the new tunnel impedes the view of the bridge: the best view is now obtained from the top of the tunnel. You can climb up to this from the embankment.

Soon we are among industry with, on our left, the Chance Glass Works where the glass for the Crystal Palace was made. The M5 motorway looms ahead: immediately before this Telford's Stewart aqueduct, constructed of brick, passes overhead. If you are short of time, you can climb up steps in the embankment to the right onto the Stewart aqueduct, over which our walk soon passes. However, a short detour is worth making in order to see Brindley's three Spon Lane locks, which are among the oldest in the country. Continue, under the aqueduct and the motorway, until you meet Brindley's original line to Wednesbury coming in from the right. Make a sharp right turn, and over a roving bridge, onto this, and then walk east up by the locks. A vast scrap heap occupies much of the area to the right. Beyond the top lock, cross the canal by a roving bridge and then return along the left hand towpath to the Stewart aqueduct, and cross this.

Our route now takes up in the direction of Oldbury and we wander round to the south underneath the M5. Originally on the left hand side of the canal, we cross to the other side near a foundry. Emerging from under the motorway, Oldbury chuch can be seen ahead, backed by the Rowley Hills through which our route will soon pass.

The canal winds back under the motorway again and we cross to the other side by a new concrete bridge. This brings us to the Titford canal, opened in 1837, along which we will make a detour. Passing a sunken narrow boat we come to the six Oldbury locks which were restored by voluntary labour in 1972-74, and which takes us up to to the highest canal in the area, 511 feet above sea level. Past the top lock, and by a pumping station, the Tat Bank feeder brings in water from Rotton Park reservoir.

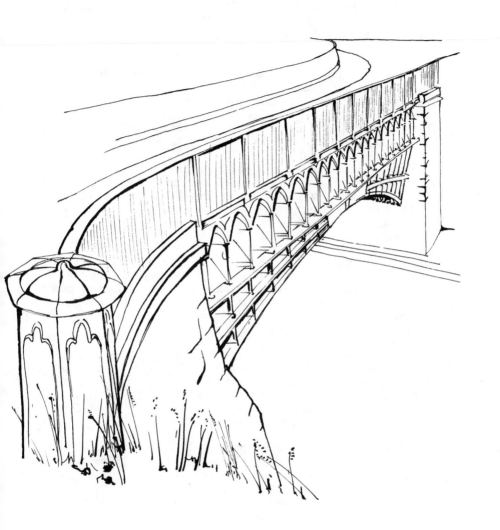

Telford aqueduct leading to the Engine Arm.

The Titford Canal takes us through Oldbury industry passing, on the left, the attractive Langley Maltings. We pass The New Navigation public house and then, after going under the A4123 and the M5, reach Titford reservoir. Buses to Birmingham, Dudley and Wolverhampton pass along the A4123 if you want to break your walk here.

Returning to our main route we meander around Oldbury, the church now reappearing on our right. Just over a mile from leaving the Titford Canal, an iron bridge takes the towpath over a branch coming up from Telford's main line, which is now about ¾ mile to the north. This branch has three locks (remember that the Smethwick locks lifted us above the Telford level), the top two locks constituting a *staircase* - that is the top gate of one lock is the bottom gate of the lock above.

After another 1¼ miles we suddenly encounter the Netherton tunnel, just after passing, on the right, the London Works Steel. Here, another branch comes in from the main line but this, instead of rising up through locks, passes underneath an aqueduct and into the tunnel. We can walk down the embankment to this, after first noting the typically Black Country skyline to the north, and the hill, through which we shall now pass, to the south.

The Netherton tunnel, opened in 1858, was the last canal tunnel to be built in Britain. It is perfectly straight, 3027 yards long, and has good towpaths on both sides. It was built to relieve pressure on the Dudley tunnel, which we shall meet later. The tunnel was originally lit by gas and later by electricity. The housing for the old generator, powered by water from the canal above, can be seen immediately under the aqueduct, and near to two canal cottages.

However, the tunnel is now unlit and you should have a good reliable flashlamp ready. Either towpath can be used, though, as both are quite wet in places, good footwear is essential. The guard rails, which look very substantial, are badly corroded further into the tunnel and, in places, missing. Do not lean on them, unless you want a swim! There are seven air shafts in the roof of the tunnel. The top and capping of one of these can be seen from the A4123.

Although there is traffic thundering overhead, no sound of this penetrates, and there is only the gentle drip of water to break the silence. In places stalactites are growing from the roof (we are passing through limestone), and there is much attractive limestone 'curtaining' on the walls. In several places streamlets of clear water penetrate the walls, making deep puddles in the towpath, the sound of running water giving advance notice of their presence.

Along the left hand path you will see numbers, increasing in fives, set into the tunnel wall. You may like to try to work out what they represent.

The tunnel emerges at Warrens Hall Park, originally a coal mining area but now a pleasant open space with the old tips grassed over. Nearby is the shell of the old pump house, with its tall chimney, which kept the mines free of water and also provided the canal with a supply of water.

Buses to Birmingham and Dudley can be found near to the entrance to Warrens Hall Park, a short walk away to the north-east. However, Netherton houses a well known Black Country pub, the Old Swan, famous for its home brewed beer. If you wish to visit this you should leave the canal a little further on at Griffin bridge and walk about half a mile north-west into Netherton. There is a bus service into Dudley from here.

Netherton Tunnel.

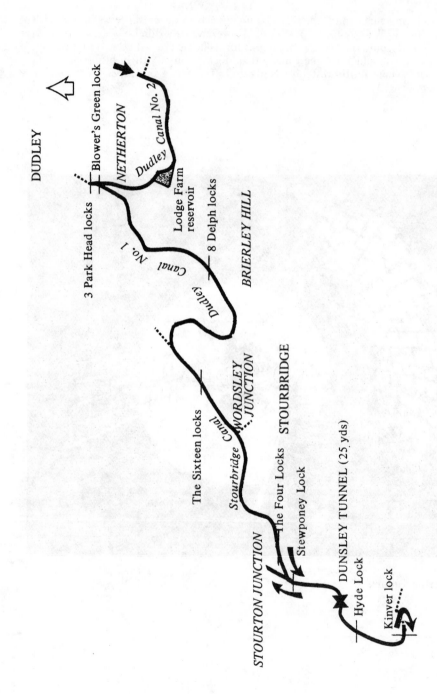

DUDLEY

Blower's Green lock

NETHERTON

Dudley Canal No. 2

3 Park Head locks

Lodge Farm reservoir

8 Delph locks

Dudley Canal No. 1

BRIERLEY HILL

WORDSLEY JUNCTION

Stourbridge Canal

STOURBRIDGE

The Sixteen locks

The Four Locks

Stewponey Lock

STOURTON JUNCTION

DUNSLEY TUNNEL (25. yds)

Hyde Lock

Kinver lock

4.   NETHERTON TUNNEL TO KINVER

The Netherton tunnel has brought us onto the Dudley No. 2 Canal which originally linked Dudley to the Worcester and Birmingham canal and provided a route for Dudley coal which by-passed Birmingham. Walking from the tunnel along the left hand towpath we go under one of a number of roving bridges that we shall see marked Toll End Works, and then over a bridge where the Dudley Canal comes in from the south-east. This originally terminated at Selly Oak after passing through the Lappal tunnel. However, the tunnel suffered continual roof falls and was closed in 1917, the line now terminating at Halesowen.

We continue in a south-westerly direction and follow a remarkable winding route as the contour canal clings to the side of a hill, which is quite steep in places. Lodge Farm reservoir soon appears on the left: this now houses the Dudley Water Ski and Yachting Club. Netherton church can be seen on a hilltop ahead. At the northern end of the reservoir is a canal cottage, in the garden of which are seen the sluices to the canal.

Immediately after, we go through a short rocky cutting. There was originally a tunnel here, but the cutting is now topped by a single span brick bridge dated 1858.

Fields now appear, those to our right below Netherton church presumably reclaimed from earlier mining operations. Cattle and horses can be seen in the fields but this rural scene suddenly changes at the deep Blowers Green lock where we encounter a concrete works. By the lock is an old pumping station.

We turn right, up the three Park Head locks and soon reach the entrance to Dudley tunnel. This was opened in 1792 and has no towpath, boats having to be legged through. We are here only about 1¼ miles as the crow flies from the Netherton tunnel although we have walked about 2¾ miles.

At the top lock there is a plaque commemorating the re-opening of the locks and tunnel on 21 April 1973. The tunnel is maintained by the Dudley Canal Trust which runs regular trips through it. The area is honeycombed with old limestone workings though some are now dangerous and blocked off.

Returning to the Blowers Green lock the winding route continues. At Round Oak we go through the massive steel works. The adjacent pub is called the Three Furnaces, worth visiting at lunchtime when it is full of steel workers.

We soon reach the eight Delph locks: up Delph Road to the left from the bottom lock is another famous Black Country pub, The Vine, which also brews its own beer. These locks are known locally as the Nine Locks, this being the number when the canal was constructed in 1779. However, there are now only eight, one having been removed when the locks were reconstructed in 1858. Although still on the BCN, these locks all have double bottom gates.

Soon, on our left, we meet a vast and barren area, perhaps soon to be put to some new use. To the left we still have a high view over the countryside even though the descents through the Park Head and Delph locks have brought us almost 100 feet down from the level at Smethwick.

As the canal bends to the north we can see the square red brick tower of Brierley Hill church. Soon we pass, on our right, a brickworks marked by two chimneys, one round and one square. Some kilns can be seen if you look carefully.

At the first of the sixteen Stourbridge locks the Fens branch doubles back to the right, beside a big works, up to the Fens Pools reservoir.

From the top lock, Wordsley church can be seen below and to the west. At lock 9 one of the old, and now preserved, kilns of the Stuart Crystal glass works appears and is reached beyond lock 13. Locks 9 and 10 are very close together, appearing at first as though they might be a staircase. However they are separate locks and the side pound can be seen on the other side of the lock keeper's cottage, which is reached by a split bridge. There is another split bridge at lock 11. At lock 12 there is a large covered wharf, originally important for the local glass industry.

The eighteen locks have carried us down 145 feet into the valley of the river Stour. We are now at Wordsley Junction where we join the Stourbridge Canal which comes in from the left. We go straight ahead, crossing the rapidly flowing Stour by an aqueduct. This is grossly polluted with industrial effluent from Halesowen, Cradley and Stourbridge.

The sounds and smells of industry seem far behind us in this beautiful part of the Staffordshire countryside. Just past the next bridge an old mill, now a farm, can be seen below on the river bank.

Approaching Stourton Junction we descend by four locks to the Staffordshire and Worcestershire canal. The waterside gardens have fully exploited the canal and the whole lock area is very attractive. There is a split bridge at the second lock. At the junction, Stourton Castle can be seen to the west.

Our main route will now take us north to Wolverhampton but we ought not to miss a delightful walk to Kinver. At the first lock (Stewponey) there is a charming circular weir which is one of the unusual features of this canal. On the far side of the lock is an old toll house, topped by a rather incongruous chimney.

We pass through the short Dunsley tunnel and along a steep wooded slope where the canal cuts through the red sandstone. By Kinver lock there is a big pumping station which brings up underground water for the public water supply.

If you want to break your journey here, a bus will take you to Stourbridge. Alternatively, if you intend to continue north and do not want to retrace your steps, the same bus will take you to Stewponey.

5. STEWPONEY TO WOLVERHAMPTON

The Staffordshire & Worcestershire Canal was built by James Brindley and the first section, from Compton to Stourport, was opened in 1771, the remainder being completed by the following year. It is a particularly fine canal for walking, mostly avoiding big towns and passing through much open country.

From the junction with the Stourbridge Canal we set off to the north after crossing bridge 33. Opposite the Stourbridge Canal there is an overflow to the river Stour. The Staffordshire and Worcestershire does not often suffer from a shortage of water, and there is usually a considerable amount coming down the Stourbridge Canal from the BCN.

After a short distance, there is a cutting into the sandstone on the opposite bank which is thought to have been used as a quarry for stone for the canal. A little further on, on the same side, is a large artificial pool, separated from the canal by an ugly fence: the origin of the pool is a mystery. Langford suggests three possibilities: first, that it was originally intended to make the link to the Stourbridge canal here rather than at Stourton; secondly, that it was a small reservoir built to conserve water; thirdly, that it was a fish pond for the nearby Prestwood Estate. If the first possibility were correct, the nature of the contours would have needed a staircase lock and Brindley may, therefore, have changed his mind in favour of the four Stourton locks. A study of the Ordnance Survey map would seem to favour this explanation - what do you think?

The canal now crosses, by an aqueduct, the river Stour, which we met earlier, carrying its load of effluent on to the Severn. There is no fishing in this river, only in the much cleaner canal which, you will see, is very popular with anglers.

A little further on, to the right, there is a cave cut into the sandstone and known as the Devil's Den. This was originally used as a boathouse by the Prestwood Estate.

This is a charming section of the canal, especially in springtime, with bluebells growing in the small wood to the left. There is a profusion of wild flowers, and the only thing to mar our pleasure is litter on the towpath.

We can see here, quite clearly, the technique of canal construction employed by Brindley on sloping ground. The soil was cut away from the higher side and dumped onto the lower, creating thereby, both the channel for the canal and the embankment. Later canal builders were less deterred by variations of contour and there are several bends on the Staffordshire and Worcestershire where one might expect that they would have cut straight through the higher ground to the right. Except in non-permeable soils, canals are sealed with clay, kneaded and *puddled* to form a watertight layer and prevent leakage.

There are several mounds of earth to be seen by the side of the towpath. These have been dumped after the dredging operations necessary to keep canals clear. You may come across a British Waterways dredger somewhere on your walk.

A little way past the Devil's Den there is a pumping station to the left, surrounded by a pleasant grassed area among the trees. We saw a pumping station earlier at Kinver and we shall meet several more on our journey northwards.

About a mile and a half from Stourton Junction we come across a ruined tower with a rubble of brickwork beside it. In the early life of the canal this was an area of considerable industrial activity. There was a canal wharf at this point and the clerk in charge lived in this 'round house'. Around, there were mills and furnaces, water power being available from the Smestow brook which runs to our left. You can see the remains of mill ponds and diversions of the brook that served the various works, but little else is left.

At Gothersley lock we start a gradual climb which will lift us 174 feet between Stourton and Aldersley. The weir at this lock is similar to the one at Stewponey although it is horseshoe shaped, not circular. We shall meet a number of variations in the pattern of weirs: the reason for this is, as yet, unknown. It has been suggested that Brindley was experimenting to find the most efficient shape, but perhaps he was just expressing a little individuality! By the side of the weir is a rake, used for clearing out debris.

Another charming charactersitic of this canal is the style of the signs on the bridges. You will have noticed that these give both the name and the number of the bridge.

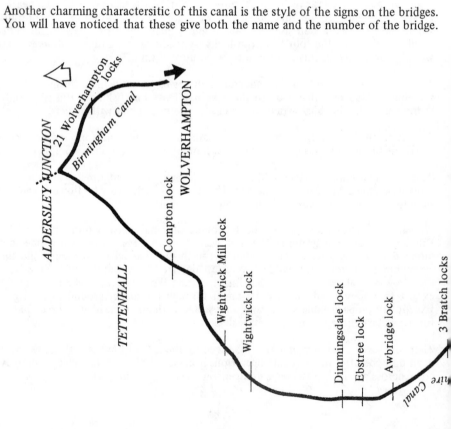

At the next lock, Rocky Lock, there is a cave cut into the sandstone which is said to have been a shelter for the navvies who built the canal. It seem rather small for this purpose so perhaps it was a stable. Just past the lock, to the right, is another pump-house. There is obviously much underground water in this area.

Beyond bridge 36 the entrance to the Ashwood basin can be seen to the right, originally built to handle coal traffic with a railway line linking it to the collieries. The basin is now used by pleasure craft.

The Navigation Inn, at bridge 37, was used by boatmen, and the old stables, now used as a store for bottles, can be seen by the canal at the rear of the inn. There is a pleasant lock keeper's cottage here.

The surroundings start to open up as the Smestow Valley widens, with a wooded area to the left. A caravan park does not improve the view. At Hinksford lock there is another variation in the pattern of the weir.

At bridge 40 we are in Swindon, where there are three pubs. Here the towpath crosses to the right to avoid an ironworks, recently demolished. It reverts to the left at the next lock. Here you will see that the two sides of what was originally a split bridge have been joined. The tow-rope marks, however, remain and their positions show the effect of the towpath changing sides.

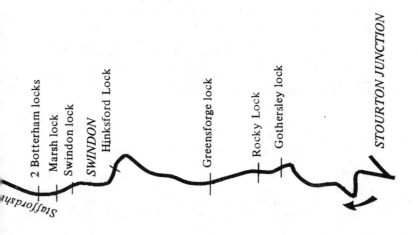

The two Botterham locks form a staircase. The lock cottage has been modernised.

We are now approaching Wombourn and the surroundings change, with some industry to the left, then becoming suburban. At bridge 45 there is a pub, the Round Oak, with draught beer but no food.

At the charmingly named Bumblehole lock there is a particularly attractive lock keeper's cottage. There is another Bumblehole at Netherton and it would be interesting to know the origin of the name. In the area there are many signs of quarrying for sand, which was used for making moulds for iron castings.

The next locks are the famous Bratch locks, certainly the most charming along this canal. The first view that we have is of the bridge and the octagonal toll-house, still in good repair. Approaching Bratch there is yet another pumping station, to the right, this one masquerading as a castle, though built in red brick.

The three Bratch locks are very closely spaced but, in spite of the British Waterways notice, they do not constitute a staircase. They are quite normal locks though the side pounds are replaced by two large ponds connected through culverts. One of the ponds is on the other side of the nearby road.

These locks replace the earlier locks built by Brindley, which are thought to have been a true staircase. Some traces of these earlier locks remain. Certainly their complexity provides ample opportunities for speculating about the various changes that might have taken place over the years.

Passing Bratch, the embankment of an old railway can be seen over to the right. We shall meet this again later. The towpath has now crossed to the right.

Awbridge lock has an extremely attractive bridge, one of the oldest along this canal.

The towpath reverts to the left at Dimmingsdale lock. All that remains of the cottage is a mound of vegetation-covered rubble. To the left is the first of the two pools of the Dimmingsdale reservoir, used for fishing and sailing. Approaching Dimmingsdale bridge is an old wharf, now used by pleasure craft. The pumping station to the right appears to have been designed by a cinema architect!

Bridges 56 and 57 both bear the name Wightwick Bridge. Approaching Wightwick lock is another wharf. Bridge 59 brings us to Compton village where there are opportunities for refreshment. The Swan public house nearby contains an interesting collection of matchbox tops on the walls.

Compton lock was the first lock to be built by Brindley on this canal. The coping stones on the far side are presumably original but those by the towpath have been replaced by blue bricks. There are towrope-worn metal bollards by the lock side and a wooden bollard just past the lock. There are two weirs, the old original circular weir and a newer one of more conventional design. The latter takes most of the water, for there is a much greater flow than there was in Brindley's day. This is due to a large outflow from Wolverhampton Sewage Works, which enters the canal above Aldersley. This is purified but still contains some trace of detergent, the foam from which you may have already noticed. This source of water kept the canal open in the great drought of 1976 when many other canals had to be closed.

Beyond Compton lock a bridge of the disused railway that we saw earlier crosses the canal. The section between Compton and Aldersley has been converted into an attractive 'walkway' (i.e. footpath). Why cannot more old railways be used in this way? There is an old station a little further on.

Bridge 63 is Dunstall Water Bridge (Tunstall on the sign) and it carries both a track and the Smestow brook over the canal, which is here passing through a cutting. It is very unusual to see a stream in an aqueduct, but when the canal was built the Smestow was being used by the mills lower down and so could not be diverted into the canal. Like the Stour, into which it flows, it is heavily polluted.

At the next bridge we reach Aldersley junction, with the Birmingham Canal to the right to which we cross. At the junction are the ruins of toll houses and various canal buildings.

We now climb up a flight of 21 locks that take us into the centre of Wolverhampton, which we can see ahead of us at the second lock (No. 20). Wolverhampton Racecourse is to our right. The third lock (No. 19) has an attractive bridge, that now goes nowhere. Almost into Wolverhampton, at lock 4, we pass the Springfield Brewery, well known locally for its Bitter. At the top lock there are two canal houses.

The area beyond the top lock has been opened up by the Corporation and converted into a pleasant grassed garden (in corporation jargon, an 'amenity area'). We are here close to Wolverhampton railway station, with buses not far away.

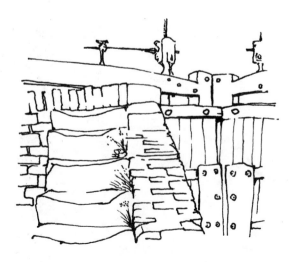

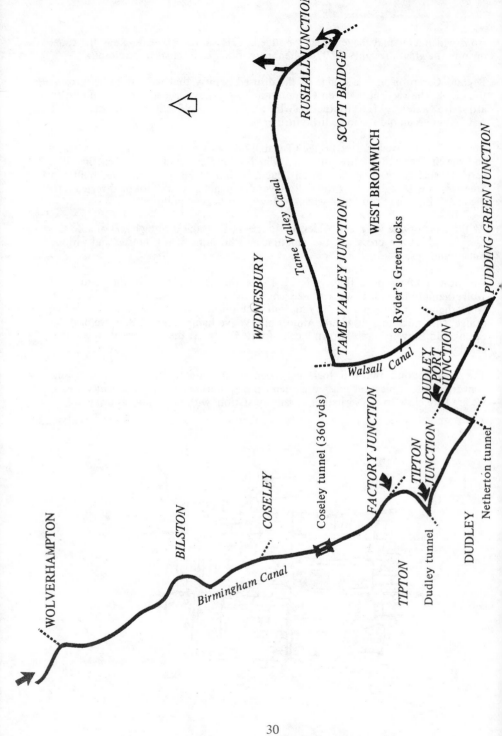

WOLVERHAMPTON

BILSTON

COSELEY

Birmingham Canal

Coseley tunnel (360 yds)

FACTORY JUNCTION

TIPTON

Dudley tunnel

TIPTON JUNCTION

DUDLEY

Netherton tunnel

DUDLEY PORT JUNCTION

Walsall Canal

8 Ryder's Green locks

WEST BROMWICH

TAME VALLEY JUNCTION

WEDNESBURY

Tame Valley Canal

PUDDING GREEN JUNCTION

RUSHALL JUNCTION

SCOTT BRIDGE

6.   WOLVERHAMPTON TO SCOTT BRIDGE

We are now, once more, in a heavily industrialised area and shall not see the open countryside again for some time.

We leave the centre of Wolverhampton in a southerly direction, under the Broad Street bridge. The towpath, which is on the left, almost immediately takes us over an arm leading to an old basin, and then under a large railway arch. We are here on a section of Brindley's Birmingham Canal which was not improved by Telford and so pursues a typical winding course. The view is similar to that we met in Birmingham, and the main interest is the signs of the former use of the canal by the factories that line the route. After a short distance the Wyrley and Essington canal goes off to the left: we have to go up to the roadway to cross the bridge over it. The Wyrley and Essington (sometimes known as the curly Wyrley) meanders away in a broadly north-easterly direction to Chasewater, and we shall meet it again shortly before we arrive here.

To the right is an old coal wharf, with sunken narrowboats, which is still used as a coal yard although the coal no longer arrives by canal.

We soon pass the British Oxygen factory to the left and then pass through a power station. The old wharfs where coal was originally delivered to the power station can be seen to the right. Just past the CEGB gates to the left a bridge takes us over an arm joining the canal to a large railway-canal interchange basin, now marked British Rail Wolverhampton Steel Terminal. It is easy to see how this originally functioned, with railway lines running alongside the basin.

The main railway line passes overhead about a mile from Broad Street, and is never far from the canal all the way to Birmingham. Just beyond the bridge the canal narrows for a *gauging stop,* where the loads carried by boats were checked for the purpose of assessing tolls. There are two canal houses here, in one of which the toll keeper would have lived.

We then pass through an engineering works in which there is, on the right, a nicely designed high chimney. Approaching the oddly spelt Jibbet Lane bridge, a large blast furnace can be seen to the right: immediately beyond a pipe bridge carrying oxygen crosses the canal. There are mains carrying oxygen, used in steel making, under the towpath, and a sign shows the position of one of the corrosion protecting anodes.

We are now, very obviously, entering a steel works and we soon get an impressive view of this to the left. The overhead crane is particularly interesting to watch and you may see it unloading iron ore from railway wagons.

The view starts to open up, the scene being dominated by two lines of vast electricity pylons. We are soon at Deepfields Junction where the Wednesbury Oak loop goes off to our left and which we cross by a roving bridge. This loop was originally the main line, before the Coseley tunnel (which we shall soon meet) was built. The southerly section of the loop has been filled in and the remaining section terminates at Bradley. Just past the loop there is a wharf to the right, where, until

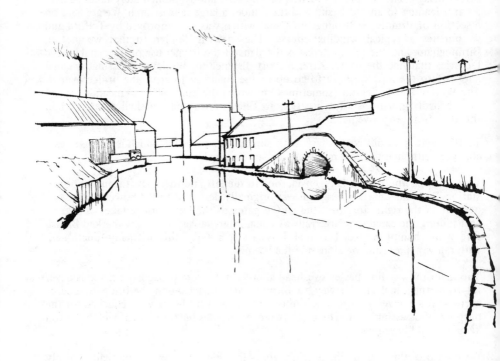

Bilston, Wolverhampton.

1977, a large fleet of working boats were based. These, sadly, are used no more for this purpose, although they will continue their useful life as pleasure craft.

We now enter a cutting which takes us into the Coseley tunnel. This is of a similar design to the Netherton tunnel with towpaths on both sides. It was opened in 1837. However it is much shorter, and much drier, than Netherton and can be walked through without a torch. Emerging from the tunnel we are in a very pleasant wooded cutting, remarkably secluded from the busy area through which it passes.

A more open region follows, where mounds from dredging operations can be seen by the towpath. These contain many coal chippings, dropped from the vast number of coal carrying boats that used to pass this way.

Soon, a metal works is reached: there is an electromagnetic crane here which you may seek picking up scrap steel to be fed into the furnaces. The square tower of Tipton church is seen ahead, and food and refreshment can be found at the Old Bush.

At Factory Junction, Telford's main line goes straight ahead down the three factory locks, but we branch off to the right along the old line. Passing under Owen Street bridge, by a canal cottage, there is a good view of the ruins of Dudley Castle on the hill to our right. Past the next bridge there is a gauging stop and canal cottage, and we then come to Tipton Junction. Here the branch to the right is the Dudley No. 1 Canal. This enters the Dudley tunnel, the other end of which we saw earlier. Before the tunnel, the canal passes through the remarkably interesting Black Country Museum, although access to the museum is possible only from the road. Ahead are the Rowley Hills on which the effects of quarrying can be seen.

About a mile from Tipton Junction we again meet the Tividale aqueduct and the Netherton tunnel. This time, however, we descend and follow to the left, the branch going north-east to meet Telford's line. On this branch there are several foundries and we can get an excellent view of casting in progress by looking through the window of the last building on the left, just a few hundred yards before Dudley Port Junction.

Arriving at the main line we cross two Toll End Works bridges and go south-east along the left hand towpath, the main railway line being immediately on our left.

A toll island, with a pipe bridge overhead, brings us to Albion Junction where the Brades branch goes off up to the right. Passing oil storage tanks we come to Albion bridge, and we cross this, past an old rope-worn bollard, onto the Walsall Canal which goes to the left. This is Pudding Green Junction. At the junction there is an old tug and some half-sunken barges.

We are now walking towards Wednesbury along the line of Brindley's original cut to the collieries. The towpath, originally on the left soon crosses to the right.

At the top of the eight Ryder's Green locks the remaining section of Brindley's Wednesbury cut goes off to the right. We continue ahead, down the locks. At the first lock, the remains of old stabling can be seen: a little further on is the Eight Locks public house. At the second lock we pass a wooden cooling tower. At the bottom lock we meet another abandoned railway interchange yard. We are now at Toll End where many of the bridges that we have seen were made. Horseley is not far away to the South-west.

Ahead are the cooling towers of Ocker Hill power station, where we turn right along the Tame Valley Canal, taking the left hand towpath.

The Tame Valley is a late canal and was built, well into the railway age, in 1844. It is very different from the earlier canals that we have walked, striding self-confidently in an almost straight line, through cuttings and along embankments, to Rushall Junction, there bending round to terminate eventually at Salford Junction. Canal building techniques had clearly developed very considerably by the time this canal was constructed: the method of balancing out soil taken from cuttings to build embankments is that used today in motorway construction.

An aqueduct takes us over the river Tame. We pass a college and playing fields on our left and go over a road by an aqueduct. As we approach a cutting the fine half-timbered Manor House can be seen to the right.

Another aqueduct takes us over a road near yet another Navigation Inn. Just before this, there is an island in the canal which permits the canal to be stopped with stop planks. Ahead can be seen the M6 motorway, which we reach soon after passing over the railway (which was here before the canal). There are particularly interesting views with motorways seemingly all around (the M5 comes in from the right) and traffic hurtling in all directions. A concrete aqueduct takes us over the motorway: this is protected by stop gates at either end, designed to swing shut in the event of a break. Whether they would do so may be questionable in view of the considerable amount of rubbish that gets dumped into this canal.

The Tame runs along to our left, then passes underneath us and round towards a sewage farm on the right. Further on we come to Rushall Junction where, under the motorways, the Rushall Canal passes to the left. We shall take this canal on the next stage of our journey, but first we continue a little further along the Tame Valley, crossing now to the right hand towpath.

We soon enter a beautiful wooded cutting with two fine bridges high overhead. The first is the Scott Bridge carrying the A4041; the second is a footbridge. A path takes us up to the A4041 where there are buses to West Bromwich, Hamstead and Sutton Coldfield. The continuing walk to Salford Junction is pleasant and you may like to do it some time. The distance is about 5½ miles.

7. RUSHALL JUNCTION TO CHASEWATER

We are now about to start on the last stage of our walk, with Chasewater about 10½ miles distant from Rushall Junction. If you left the last section at the Scott bridge, this is probably the best place to rejoin, retracing your steps back from there to Rushall Junction.

The Rushall Canal goes due north and, from its straightness, is obviously a late canal. It was opened in 1847, three years after the Tame Valley Canal. We very soon leave behind the noise of the motorway and find ourselves in pleasant green fields.

At Biddlestone bridge you will see the remains of a support set into sandstone on the corner of the bridge. You may like to speculate on what this was: the answer will be found a little further on.

We soon pass, on our right, the Shustoke Farm sports ground of the University of Aston, and then come to the first of the six Rushall locks which will lift us about 65 feet. These are the last locks that we shall meet on our walk.

At lock 6 there is a toll house, and, between locks 6 and 5, a lock keeper's house. This is larger, and less interesting, than the older cottages that we have seen. At the bridge to lock 3 you should, perhaps, be able to obtain the answer to the question that was posed at Biddlestone bridge.

At lock 3 there is another lock keeper's cottage with a garden by the lockside.

We are here in the residential suburb of Great Barr and we pass through pleasant modern housing. The owners have made good use of, to the right, the canal bank and, to the left, the embankment. This is an excellent example of what can be done with a canal in a residential area. You may have noticed a counter-example a little further back where, because houses were separated from the embankment by a fence, the area had become a rubbish tip.

Locks 1 and 2 are separated by just over a mile from lock 3 and we are now out into pleasant open country again. To the north-west are the cooling towers of Walsall power station. In the towpath can be seen many coal chippings, for this was an important route for the shipment of coal from the many former collieries. At the top lock is the headquarters of Longwood Boat Club.

Beyond the top lock the canal takes on a different appearance, winding around in sharp contrast to its earlier straightness. We are here on a much earlier section of the canal, opened in 1800 as an extension of the Wyrley and Essington Canal that we saw in Wolverhampton.

Passing a sign marking a footpath to St Michael's church, which can be seen through the trees to the left, we cross the railway by an aqueduct. The next bridge is the modern Daw End bridge (1971) where there is access to pubs.

35

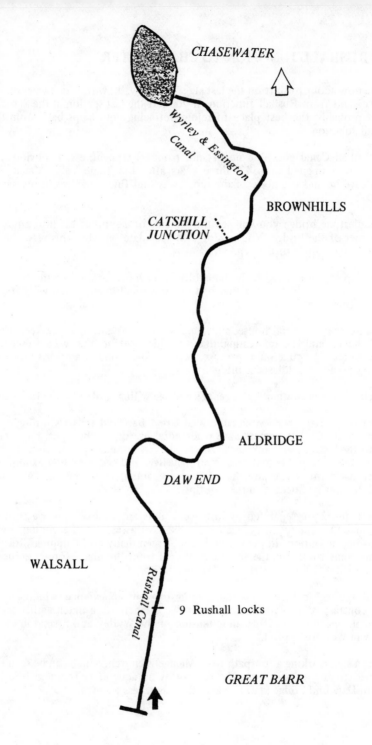

CHASEWATER

Wyrley & Essington Canal

BROWNHILLS

CATSHILL JUNCTION

ALDRIDGE

DAW END

WALSALL

Rushall Canal

9 Rushall locks

GREAT BARR

The canal twists around Daw End in a wide loop, and then brings us to Aldridge where there is a pocket of modern light industry. To the right we pass a big international road/sea container dept: it is interesting to try to work out from which countries the various containers originate. Beyond a fuel oil depot and then a bridge, signs of old mine workings can be seen to the left.

After passing a concrete works we reach an area in which there have been extensive clay workings, above which the canal is precariously poised. There are still two brick works here, one of which is alongside a road over to our left. A prominent landmark is a tall ruined building which presumably once housed pumping equipment. Some of the old clay pits are now used for the disposal of toxic waste and to the left behind a high wire fence you will see the tanks that hold some of this.

Refreshments can be obtained at the next road bridge (dated 1883 on the far side), where there is a large mock-something-or-other hotel and a real beer pub, the Horse and Jockey.

After passing under Walsall Wood bridge, Walsall Wood church is passed on the right. Approaching the next bridge you will see pigeons in the garden to the left, for pigeon racing is a popular pastime in the West Midlands.

Beyond the bridge, and where we swing to the north, a railway once crossed the canal. A road bridge over this railway can be seen to the right, but little else remains. However, a little further on, it is possible to see, over to the left by some houses, the remains of a bridge where the railway went over another line which also crossed the canal.

Ahead, to the north, can be seen the high ground of Cannock Chase. By the towpath are old dredging heaps containing coal chippings: some newer heaps contain a wider variety of more exotic rubbish. Here you will see numbers painted by the canal bank: these mark out fishing positions for the local angling clubs, for this is a clear, unpolluted canal, good for fish. There are many remains of old mines and clay workings in this area.

Some tall blocks of flats overlook Catshill Junction where we meet the Wyrley and Essington which comes in from the left. Before the junction there is a gauging stop and, to the left, an area that has suffered from subsidence. We cross a roving bridge and walk east, now along the Wyrley and Essington Canal. Past the first bridge we have good agricultural land on our right and housing on our left.

We soon meet an old flour mill, now a toy factory, on the left. A red stain on the wall, around an extractor fan, is due to paint spraying.

A roving bridge (Horseley Works 1829) takes us across a branch which originally linked to the Coventry Canal. This was closed in 1954. After crossing the railway we pass under the Freeth bridge, which carries the Roman Watling Street. The original bridge is sandwiched between two new extensions on either side. Past the next bridge is an old coal wharf, with the shutes used for loading narrow boats still intact. Coal was brought here by rail from the Cannock Chase coalfields and the remains of the railway can be seen. Across the road (Wharf Road) are the remains of an old level crossing gate, and over to the south-east is a cutting. To the north-west, by Chasewater, is another cutting.

A short section of canal now takes us to Chasewater. This section was only opened in 1850, replacing an earlier feeder channel from the reservoir. Ahead is the dam which encloses the reservoir. Water enters at the very end of the canal and also, when the water level is sufficiently high, along an overflow channel on the left. At the end of the canal a track goes up to the top of the dam, along which you can walk. Chasewater is popular for water sports and you will probably see yachting and water ski-ing.

So, you are now at the end of the walk. Unlike the Pennine Way there is no free pint of beer for you from the author; and if you want a nice badge you will have to walk the Offa's Dyke Path. But you have had, we hope, an enjoyable walk, you have seen some attractive country, and you know more about the canals and their relationship to the geography, the history and the economy of the region. Now to return home and, perhaps, to plan more canal exploration - such as from Kinver to Stourport, a remarkable eighteenth century town that owes its entire existence to the canal; from Lapworth to Stratford on Avon; from Lapworth to Warwick or beyond (perhaps to London?); to explore further the Black Country; maybe to repeat this walk but in the reverse direction: the possibilities are many and varied. For the present, however, some rest and refreshment. A short walk directly south from the dam, and then left around a sports stadium, will bring you to a pub; and nearby are buses to Birmingham, Walsall and Cannock.

Clay workings, Aldridge.

38

THE NAVIGATION WAY. Table of distances.

Canal		Miles
Birmingham & Fazeley	Birmingham, Gas Street	0
Grand Union	Salford Junction	3½
	Bordesley Junction	5¾
	Olton	10
	Solihull (B4012)	13½
	Knowle	16½
Stratford-on-Avon	Kingswood Junction	20
	Hockley Heath	22¾
	Shirley	28
Worcester & Birmingham	Kings Norton	32
	Selly Oak	34½
Birmingham	Birmingham, Gas Street	37¼
	Smethwick Junction	40½
	Spon Lane Junction	43½
	Oldbury Junction	44¾
	Titford Reservoir	45½
	Netherton Tunnel	47¾
Dudley No. 2	Park Head Junction	52
	The Delph	54¼
Stourbridge	Wordsley Junction	57
Staffs & Worcs.	Stourton Junction	59
	Kinver	60½
	Swindon	64¾
	Compton	71
Birmingham	Aldersley Junction	73¼
	Wolverhampton	75¼
	Deepfields Junction	78½
	Factory Junction	79
Walsall	Pudding Green Junction	83½
Tame Valley	Tame Valley Junction	85½
	Rushall Junction	88¾
	Scott Bridge	89½
Rushall	Daw End	92½
Wyrley & Essington	Catshill Junction	97½
	Chasewater	100

In working out this table, the distances along the three extensions from the main route - to Titford reservoir, to Kinver and to Scott Bridge - have been counted in one direction only.

FURTHER READING

The books listed below have been selected to cover various aspects of canals — routes, scenery and history. But many other excellent titles are to be found in bookshops and libraries.

Nicholson's Guides to the Waterways (British Waterways Board). Volumes 1 - 4 of this series have been my constant companions when walking the towpaths. They are illustrated by strip maps and are a mine of useful information.

J I Langford: *Towpath guide No. 1. The Staffordshire and Worcestershire Canal* (Goose & Son). An extremely detailed study of almost everything that can be seen from the towpath of this charming canal.

Charles Hadfield: *The canals of the West Midlands* (David and Charles). A very readable history that includes all the canals of the Navigation Way.

Anthony Burton: *The Canal Boatmen 1760-1914* (Manchester University Press). The lives of the men, and the women, who worked the narrow boats in the Midlands.

Lewis Braithwaite: *Canals in Towns* (A & C Black). The existing and potential uses of urban canals. Contains a very useful collection of canal walks.